The 25

▮▮▮▮▮▮ The 25

25 Strategies to Teach Your Child About Money

By Raeshal Solomon

Copyright © 2018 by Raeshal Solomon

All rights reserved. No part of this book may be reproduced in any form or by any electronic or mechanical means, including information storage and retrieval systems, without written permission from the publisher, except by a reviewer who may quote passages in a review.

Published by Raeshal Solomon
Editor Julie Breihan
ISBN

Printed in the United States of America

Dedication

To all the parents out there like me struggling to be the better parent you can.

Thank you to the parents taking time out of your busy schedule to read this book. I know that being a parent can be hard at times. We all know there is no manual on how to raise your child.

At the end of the day as parents we use examples from our parents, we watch, ask advice from friends and family, or we go to the experts for different issues and knowledge.

I know with all the other subjects out in the world we teach our children; money may not seem to be as necessary, but it is because cash touches all factors of your life as an adult. And it will affect theirs as well. Once again thank you for taking time to learn from me.

Confessions of a financially broke mother

As I write this book, I am the proud mother of two, but when my financial journey began over eighteen years ago, I was twenty-something and broke. One of the reasons was because when I was six months old, I was diagnosed with a chronic illness know as Sickle Cell Anemia.

Although this illness played a significant part in the challenges of my financial life, it wasn't the only reason I was broke. The main factor that contributed to my economic problems was not a lack of knowledge or a lack of income; it was lack of self-control.

I didn't always have the discipline I needed to make the changes in my financial life that were vital. As a young person, no one ever gave me any advice about money, so I went with the flow. Money moved like water in my house. As quickly as it came, it went. And I didn't save any of it.

I worked all my high school and college years while raising my younger brother. I signed up for my first credit card at age eighteen after class one day. A group of young people were offering hats, T-shirts, and sunshades to fill out an application, so I did.

In college, my mind-set toward money was that it could get me the things I wanted to buy. I worked and used my earning and my college loan refunds to buy stuff. I used my student loan refund to buy my second car. My mom had bought me a car when I was seventeen, but it was twenty years old and a piece of crap,

so I convinced myself that I needed a new one. The worst part of this story was that I had grants and scholarships and didn't even need the school loans. But no one ever taught me to manage my money, so I just did what I could to survive.

When I was a teen I didn't receive financial advice from family, so I created a "List of Don'ts."

I am sure you are wondering what that is. Well, I had created a list of things I thought were terrible or dangerous, things I considered mistakes or bad habits, mistakes my parents and other family members had made that I didn't want to repeat. I knew that I didn't want to be poor, and I knew that I didn't want to have children at a young age.

Using my list of don'ts is how I made a lot of money decisions in my youth. My list was a good start, but it did not help with every situation. For example, I knew I didn't want to be poor, but I didn't know how to invest to become rich.

I didn't want to have children at a young age, but I didn't know to save the money I wasn't spending because I didn't have children.
.

Brilliant Twenty-somethings

In my brilliant twenty-somethings, I had plans for my life and my money. I got my first apartment at twenty while I was still in college. At first, I had many different roommates, some dependable, some not. After a while, I got tired of dealing with others, and their friends, so I got a one bedroom and did what I could to make the payments. My brother moved in and crashed on the couch. It was small, but it was mine. But I graduated college with staggering debt, and it only got worst.

I got my first salary job about a month after college graduation. I was making more money than I ever had, but still, I had no clue what to do with it. I had a ton of debt, but my credit score was not horrible. And after about eight months of focusing on improving my rating, I increased my credit score. I bought my first house when I was twenty-six.

Boy, was that stupid. I lost my job nine months after I bought the house.

It was 2007, and everyone was getting fired. The economy was crashing, and I had no backup plan, no second job, and no emergency fund. I was young, scared, and embarrassed. By this time a few of my family members had started depending on me for financial help, help that I could no longer provide.

I didn't know who to ask about my current financial situation; everyone I knew was broke, poor, or secretive about their money.

I applied for unemployment, and because of my Sickle Cell, I also asked for SSI disability. I got approved for both. Now I had money coming in, but it was barely enough to cover the mortgage. So once again I had to get roommates, and once again some were financially dependable and stayed around for a while, and some were not and were evicted.

For two years I cried in secret while living check to check and negotiated with the mortgage company not to foreclose. At this time in my life, I was so worried and stressed, but I learned so much about laws, money, and the art of negotiating it's unbelievable.

From 2007 to 2009, I was unemployed, but in late 2009, I went to a job fair and got a job as an assistant manager at a gas station. The pay was minimal, but it was a job, and it felt good to be working again.

I shined at my job, always doing a little extra, and my hard work paid off. A recruiter from a local restaurant chain noticed me and hired me into their management training program. Once again, I had a great job making over $50,000 a year, but I didn't know what to do with it.

Six months later training was over, and I had to move closer to my new store, so I rented out my house and moved. I worked long hours. The work was hard, and I would often go to work sick because of my Sickle Cell, but the money was good.

I meant a guy while I was in management training. He was cute, funny, and understood my busy hours. After being in that relationship for a year, I got pregnant, but it was clear that we had different goals and had to part ways.
It Does Get Better

It Does Get Better

It's 2012, at thirty-two years old, I was in over $400,000 in debt, unemployed, single, homeless, and pregnant with my first child. But I struggled tooth and nail to get out of debt. As I write this story, it's 2018, and I'm not debt-free, but I'm getting close.

I am sure you are wondering how I turned my financial life around. But first, let me tell you just a little more. I had to quit my job when I found out I was pregnant.

I was high risk due to the Sickle Cell and because I had a miscarriage when I was six months pregnant a few years earlier. I was single because the guy didn't want to be a father at that time.

I was homeless because I had no income and I was renting my house to good tenants. Now, I know you think I should have kicked them out or moved in with them, but I decided that my pain was not their problem. And I couldn't afford the mortgage.

So How Did I Fix It

I moved in with family to get me back on my feet. I went back on Social Security Disability. I guess that was something like a security umbrella. Don't get me wrong, it was hard to acquire. I had to fight for months to get it back. It wasn't a lot, but it helped, and once my son was three months old, we moved to our own place.

One day when my son was about nine months old, I stood staring out a window as tears ran down my face. I could hear my baby boy playing on the couch behind me.

It was amazing to me that he could be so happy while at the same time I was so frustrated. I had just gotten off the phone with a disrespectful debt collector, and at that moment I vowed not to let my kids know the level of financial illiteracy that I struggled with.

At that moment I knew that my children would never know that feeling of lack. Not just lack of money, but lack of money knowledge.
At that moment I changed my mind-set about money. It would no longer be what I used to buy what I wanted. Money is a tool. A tool I was going to learned how to use.

See, I had been reading money books for years, but I wasn't using what I had learned. So, I prayed more. I needed strength, and praying was the only way I knew how to get it. I grew up praying my pains away as a child, and now I was praying away a different kind of pain.

I changed the people I spent time with. A lot of my friends didn't know anything about money. And they spent a lot of time spending money they didn't have. I couldn't continue doing the same things I had done in the past; it was time for something new.

I surrounded myself with people with the same goals. My church was offering a financial literacy class, so I joined it. I had the opportunity to meet new likeminded people. To be honest, I knew most of what we learned in the class, but what I realized was that I wasn't using any of it.

The time for inaction was over. I had my son, and I needed to do better. I became more disciplined with my money. I did a cash audit on myself. I wrote down every dollar I spent for two months. I used those numbers to help me create my monthly budget and debt-snowball plan.

I got a copy of my credit report, so I could call the collectors and negotiate my payment plans. I changed my shopping habits. I stopped carrying my debit cards and for a while used only cash. I read every book and online article and listened to every podcast I could find about money, and I still do.

During this time, I was also blessed with my second son. He is my biological nephew, but I have full custody of him. I got him when he was two years old after he was taken from his mother. My brother, his father, thought I would be the best guardian for him.

I am glad I had already started working on my financial situation because he came with nothing. He is only two months younger then my son, so they shared clothes and diapers until I could buy him some of the things he needed.

Now My Life is Different

It's incredible to me now that I lived through all this. When I give people advice about what they can do to change their lives and I get excuses in return, I laugh inside. I always think,

If you knew my whole story, maybe you would change your tone, but I don't say anything; I listen. I have learned it's all about your mind-set. My journey has not been easy, but I learned from my mistakes, and I acted to make different choices the next time.

True, my parents had never taught me about money. However, that is no excuse for me to not teach children. My children are only five, but I have been teaching them using the techniques in this book since they were ages one and two.

Behavioral specialists say that when you are asking a child to do something for the first time, you can't just tell them what to do. You must explain it to them in detail.

You can't tell them to clean their room and expect them to clean it like you would. You must do it with them and explain the steps. For example, you let them know they need to fold their underclothes, hang up their shirts, put all the toys in the blue bin, etc. I take that same approach to teaching my children about money. I taught myself about money, then I taught my children, and now I am teaching the children of the world.

I wrote my first children's financial literacy book the day after that call from the disrespectful collector. Since then I have written twenty-five more. My books are called the My Little Banker series. I use fun, colorful stories that are easy to read and that contain a money lesson.

I also go around the country teaching kids about money, and I teach parents how, what, and when to teach their children about money. I am happy to be in my purpose teaching people from my pain. Money is no longer something I don't understand; now it's a tool I use to grow my career and my legacy.

Read on to learn what I have been teaching kids from all over the country about money for the past five years.

"By changing nothing, nothing changes." —Tony Robbins

Loving Parents

In this book I mention a few times how my parents didn't take the time to teach me about money. Don't get me wrong, my parents were great parents.

As I mentioned, I was a sickly child. I'm sure they just felt blessed on my well days and miserable on my sick days. They have raised my siblings and me to be wonderful, loving people. My parents struggled financially as well, although they both worked.

Money wasn't a fun topic in our household and surely not something to speak to the kids about. I don't blame them for my mistakes. As a parent, I know there is so much to teach children that some things fall through the cracks.

I also know that their parents didn't speak to them about money either. They had no examples to pull from when it came to financial literacy for themselves or their children.

As your reading this, stop and think about your parents for a minute. Did they discuss money with you? What was the money language around your home? Was money a topic for discussion around the dinner table?

Start early

No matter your child's age, you should start teaching them about money now. I am sure if you are the parent of a one-year-old you may think it's too early, but it's not. When my son was one, I started teaching him simple money phrases like, "Money goes in the bank" and "Nothing is free but love." Once my sons were old enough to repeat the statement "Money goes in the bank," we started putting money in their piggy banks.

One summer my boys went to my sister's house for a visit. After they were there for about three days, she called me and said, "Sis, what are you doing with these boys? Every time they see or find money they want to put it in the bank.

So now we have a jar full of change in the kitchen on the counter." I started laughing and then I replied, "I am just teaching them about money." The boys were almost three at the time. Like any other subject, money management can be learned.

If you're the parent of a teenager, you may think it's too late to teach them about money, but once again, it's not. I speak to so many teens who wish their parents would teach them more about money.

All things start with a simple conversation. A key point to remember is not to make assumptions about what your child can learn or about what they may already know.

Learning about money is a building skill. Once you understand one thing, you add more. Think of it like math: once you learn to add and subtract, then you learn multiplication and division. The sooner you start, the easier it will become for your little banker to master this skill.

"Train up a child in the way he should go, and when he is old he will not depart from it." — Proverbs 22:6

Show Your Child What to Do

People of all ages learn from their experiences. Remember that children learn in four different ways. The four ways are sight (visual), audio (listening), physical (do it), reading and writing. Showing your child what you do with your money will help them remember and learn faster. Use real-life opportunities to teach them money concepts like saving, giving, and spending.

Whether you know it are not, you are a living example to your children. Their lives will mirror your life in many ways. If you're not proud of your money habits, you can change them. Or at least you can tell your children that in this one area of money you are an example of what not to do.

Help your children learn from your mistakes. This will require some transparency from you, the parent. However, it can be done.
One mother of five I know goes weekly grocery shopping with her kids. They split up into two groups and have a shopping contest.

The rules of the contest are that whichever group finishes first and saves the most money wins a prize. The prize is usually something small, like getting sorbet.

She says because of the goal of the game her kids don't ask for things not on the list. She also has them put in their suggestions when she is creating the list, so they feel included in the process.

This single mother is teaching her children how to eat healthy and save money with coupons, and they're having fun as a family.

"The greatest mistake you can make in life is to be continually fearing you will make one." — Elbert Hubbard

Let Your Child Create a Budget

You may be surprised, but even young children can create a budget. Parents should have their child create a wish list of toys, clothes, or whatever they want to purchase on a piece of paper. Once a list is created, find prices for all the items on the list.

I would even suggest that you have them prioritize the list from most important to least important. Or from cheapest to most expensive. This exercise will help them when it comes to writing a budget as an adult.

Now that your child knows what they want like bikes, game systems, or a doll and how much it all costs, it's time to plan ways for them to make money. Then let them make purchases from their wish list with their own money.

When my niece was eighteen, she called me for some advice. She wanted to move out of her parents' house, but she wasn't sure what she needed to do. We talked for an hour, and I gave her homework. Her homework was to create a moving budget.

She had to find an apartment complex where she wanted to move and ask about cost of rent and deposits. Then she had to call the light and water company and call the moving truck company for a quote. Once she had all her numbers and created her budget, she called me back.

After seeing all the numbers and knowing how much she made from work, she decided not to move because she didn't think she could afford it. I think she made the best decision for her situation at the time.

Now she is a junior in college making good grades, lives on campus, and is not stressed over bills.

Go to mylittlebanker.com/resources for a budget.

"An investment in knowledge pays the best interest." —Benjamin Franklin

Have a Home Store

For parents on a budget, you can always be creative and create a home store. Have your children earn paper money that you create. They can use that money to buy snacks or services.

Services could be things like one day of no chores or one day of not cleaning their rooms. They can also use the house money to buy things like TV time, tablet time, and video game system time. Your family can be as creative as you want with the products and services your house money can buy.

Using this technique with siblings will be helpful because they can learn to trade and negotiate with one another. Negotiating skills are very important and often one of the topics I teach in my "Women, Wealth, and Wine" workshops.

I suggest you encourage some negotiation between you and the child or between siblings to help build this skill. Though you may want to set up some rules for the house money, so the older siblings don't take advantage of the younger ones.

"If men liked shopping, they'd call it research."
— Cynthia Nelms

Kids Can Save Too

For younger children, let them save at home in a clear jar. The reason for that is because kids like to watch their money grow. It becomes a game to children to see how fast they can make their money increase. The point of saving at home is so that children can understand the concept of letting their money rest. Just because you have money doesn't mean you need to spend it.

As they watch their money grow in the clear jar, you will notice that they will get excited about the savings process. If you have more than one child, you may even notice a little competition growing between them.

Then once there is a decent amount of money in the jar, have them move it over to a local bank. You will have little savers before you know it. But if you don't want to open a bank account, that's okay. The point of all of this is to teach them knowledge that they can use as adults.

Every other year it's our family goal to go to Disney World. This year the boys are five, and they understand what money is and how to use it. At the beginning of the year, I told them we would be going to Disney World, but they had to help pay for it.

I took a clear mason jar and covered it with some Disney stickers. We call it our family Disney jar, and the boys know that the money in the jar is used to go to Disney World. Then we went to the family calendar in the kitchen and circled the three days of the trip and I added Disney stickers to it as well.

For the past six months, every time they get money for birthdays, Christmas, or anywhere else, they can choose to put the money in the Disney jar or their piggy bank. They almost always want to put the money in the Disney jar.

I have not added any money to the jar; it's all from them, and there's about $150 in there. That may not sound like a lot, but they are *five*! I am so proud of them because they are learning patience and saving for a goal.

"Too many people spend money they earned to buy things they don't want to impress people that they don't like." —Will Rogers

Teach Them Money and Manners

A As you wait in the line at stores and shopping centers, let your children help you unload the cart and give them the money to pay the cashier. Allowing them to pay not only gives them a better understanding of what things cost but also helps them learn that things are not free. Kids need to understand at a young age that money is exchanged in many forms to buy almost everything.

I pride myself on teaching my boys to be little gentlemen. They open doors for me and other women and say "yes, sir" and "no, ma'am." I often get compliments on my boys because of their manners. I sometimes remind them that manners will help get them further in life.

Teaching my sons to help me in the store is just as much about money as it is about manners. It doesn't matter if it's my money or their money; they know we are paying for the services and goods. I have also used opportunities of shopping to explain what stealing is and why it's a bad thing to do. Look for chances to tie in money into daily conversations.

"It does not matter how slowly you go as long as you do not stop." — *Confucius*

Create a Savings Club

I If your child doesn't have siblings, or if your children are years apart, it may be a good idea to get some other parents involved. Start a savers club for the kids.

Having friends who are doing the same things as them will make the process fun, create great memories, and give them some accountability. It may also make the learning process easier. Consider even having them save for a group goal like a pizza party or a movie night.

Turning saving into a group activity will make it easier to explain investments to them as they get older. Being in a saving club for a kid is like being in a mutual fund for adults. It's just a group of people pooling their money together for faster growth in value.

"Accountability breeds response-ability."
—*Stephen R. Covey*

Open Their Own Bank Account

Once their clear jar is full or close to full of money, let them take the jar to the bank. Make sure this trip to the bank is a fun event. Make the whole event a game and be over-animated at each step of the process. Give high fives and tell them that they are doing a good job as they put coins in the machine or hand the bank teller money.

Of course, you will guide them through the process at the bank, but you want them to do all the work. If there are coins, let them put the coins in the machine. Have your child give the teller the cash and coin ticket and get the receipt. Before you leave the bank, review the receipt with them to teach them to check for mistakes.

I started doing this with my boys when they were two years old. They love putting coins in the coin machines. We have been putting money in their accounts twice a year for about three years.

I recently had a conversation with one of my sons because he made the statement that he didn't like putting money in the big bank.

I asked him why, and he said, "Because once I put it in there, I can't take it out." I had never thought about it, but they had never made a withdrawal.

We had only made deposits, so he thought the money was all gone. I explained to him that we could go and get the money whenever we needed it but that we didn't need it right now, so it was just sitting in there waiting on him.

Then he asked how that all worked, and I told him they had his name and every time he added money, they add that amount to his name. Then he understood. Note: this is my son who likes to spend money. Guess it's time to make a withdrawal. #teachingmoment #mlbmoment

"Independence is essential for permanent but fatal to immediate success." —Samuel Butler

Write a Paper Check

You might be surprised, but I have met many teenagers who don't know how to write a check. Kids as young as seven years old should be able to write a check. At the bare minimum, they need to understand what to write in each field: name, memo, amount, etc. A child also needs to be able to identify the routing number and account number.

I can still remember the feeling of frustration from writing my first few paper checks. I know in this age of technology writing a paper check sounds crazy, but it's still a useful skill.

And it doesn't take very long to teach. Even electronic checks have the same look and feel as paper checks. So, have your child write a few for practice. You may want to show them how to fill out a money order as well.

Go to mylittlebanker.com/resources for a paper check template.

"If you truly want to be respected by people you love, you must prove to them that you can survive without them." —Michael Bassey Johnson

Embrace Technology

Whether you are comfortable with it or not, we are in an age of technology. Kids today have no problem handling technology and banking this way will feel natural to him or her. Children of today will never know a time before online banking, or cell phones, or tablets. Using technology will be one of the easier ways to teach your child about money.

Let them see their transactions on a phone, tablet, or computer and ask them questions to help them think about what it is they are looking at. For example, if there is a transaction for $4 on their statement, ask where they spent the $4 and what they bought.

Maybe they bought an ice cream cone from the ice cream shop, and the total was $4. Helping to identify transactions and knowing their current balance will be one more useful skill as they get older. This is also a great opportunity to teach them the differences between pending and processed transactions.

Processed transactions are transactions that have already come out of your account. A pending transaction is money that is being held but is not out of your account yet.

Sometimes places like gas station may only hold $1 for a $25 charge. Not paying attention to their account and their numbers can cause them to overdraft if they are not careful.

"Technology is just a tool. In terms of getting the kids working together and motivating them, the teacher is the most important." — *Bill Gates*

Read Books with Them

Every year there are more and more books coming out that teach children about money. Gone are the days of using books that don't relate to today's society or culture.

It's easy to go online and find e-books and physical books to help. For new age books with money, lessons visit my website at MyLittleBanker.com.

The books that are currently for purchase on my site are for children ages ten and under; however, I am always adding more. Each book teaches on a different money concept like saving, giving etc. Remember that child learn in different ways, so if you have a child who loves to read books that would be a great way to help them.

There are also many benefits to having your children read books, like exercising the brain, getting better at reading, and learning new vocabulary words.

"You cannot open a book without learning something." — *Confucius*

Let's Play Bank

Your children may often play school, cops and robbers, and doctor and patient. Why not encourage them to play bank teller and customer? At your local dollar store, you can find cheap fake paper money, cash registers, and toy vaults.

They can make deposits and withdrawals and even fill out checks and bank slips. This also gives you the opportunity to teach them what the words *deposit,* and *withdrawal* means.

This tip is especially helpful if you are a parent on a budget and you don't have real money to give your child to learn with. Don't forget the point of all of this is to have the conversations that will reflect in their action as adults.

"Banking is necessary; banks are not." —Bill Gates

Play Store

After playing bank, your children can play store. It can be whatever type of store they want. They can pretend to spend some of the money they got from the bank and make small purchases.

Playing store with your children can be a wonderful experience. You may even be surprised by how well they learn to negotiate. There are many money lessons in playing store.

A few lessons you can teach while playing store are supply and demand, added value, importance of good customer service, getting return clients, and finding value. Just be creative; you never know what your child can learn.

If you think of another money lesson that kids can learn from playing store share with me at info@mylittlebanker.com.

"We always hold hands. If I let go, she shops." — *Henry Youngman*

Do Chores

Every parent has heard this tip before, but it's still important to say. Doing chores is a useful money teaching tool. You can use chores to teach about money subjects like paydays, paychecks, negotiation of wages, and of course responsibility.

Children need to understand that money comes from some form of work.
Having a chore chart makes the process of chores easier. Chore charts give everyone a point of reference when it comes to doing the work. This way one child can't blame the other for not doing what needs to be done.

Let's be honest, as parents we are busy and tired; we don't care who washes the dishes. All we care about is if the dishes get washed. So, having a chart with clear responsibilities keeps everyone on track.

Go to mylittlebanker.com/resources for a chore chart.

There is also opportunity here to talk about being an entrepreneur and not having to work for others. The earlier your child can figure out if they like others telling them how much they make or when they must work, the better it will be for them.

Maybe they realize that they don't like that, and they want to be their own boss.

For more about kidpreneurs, listen to my podcast PodKash Kids on podkashkids.com

"Choose a job you love, and you will never have to work a day in your life." — Confucius

Buy Paper Money

If your child is very young, like ages three to six, I would use paper money to help them learn how to count money. You can use it to play games, play bank, and when playing store.

Counting money can be tricky or very confusing to some kids because of the different sizes and dollar amounts. However, because paper bills and plastic coins look like real money, it can be used as a hands-on tool to teach kids.

One of my sons loves to learn and quickly understood that a quarter is twenty-five cents. My other son must be shown. Your children will learn at different rates, and that's okay.

Just remember that kids use the four different ways to learn. Find out which learning style works best for your child and use that information to your advantage.

"There are no keys to success—only tools." — Criss Jami

"Remember this—you can't serve God and Money, but you can serve God with money." — Selwyn Hughes

Don't Stop with Tithes Make Donations

You don't have to buy things and give cash to learn to be a giver. Your little banker can give their time to people in need. They can help at a food bank, a hot kitchen, or a pet shelter. Time is just as valuable as money.

They can give old toys or clothes to the Salvation Army. Or even better, they can give away new stuff.

This is another place where you can show by example. We are moving, and I am teaching my children to give away some of their belongings. And to be honest, they don't like it.

But if I don't show them now with actions, they will feel entitled, and maybe a little spoiled, as adults. Think of an entitled person you know. How do they treat others? Do you want your child acting like them?

"No person was ever honored for what he received. Honor has been the reward for what he gave." — Calvin Coolidge

Buying Friend's Gifts Can be Fun

You can have your child save their money to buy a birthday or holiday present for a friend or sibling. This gift-giving exercise can open all kinds of money topics for discussion.

You will have the opportunity to talk about giving, saving, the cost of gifts, and the value of money. It will be interesting to see what kinds of gifts your kids pick when they must use their own money.

I have learned that while some children only focus on themselves, kindhearted children will go out of their way to buy something nice for their friends and family.

My sons are so funny to me. They are the same age, but they act completely different. My one son is a saver but the best gift giver ever. He always thinks about the person and tries to buy or make something very personal and meaningful to that person.

My other son, the spender, couldn't care less about what to give others. It's all about what he can get out the deal. I am sure you can imagine me giving him the same lectures repeatedly about selflessness and selfishness.

Share a picture and a story of a gift on social media that your child purchased for someone with the hashtag #mylittlebanker so we can join in the conversation.

"The value of a man resides in what he gives and not in what he is capable of receiving." —Albert Einstein

Get a Job Outside the Home

Teens should get a job to learn about paychecks, taxes, and hourly wages. This is a great way to teach about opportunity cost. Opportunity cost is the opportunity lost by buying one thing over another.

For example, if your kid is saving for a bike, but they keep buying snacks with their money, then they are losing the opportunity to purchase the bike. Or the chance to buy the bike faster. In other words, this will hopefully help them to learn self-control with their money.

Getting your first job can teach you about so much more than money. You learn about schedules, time management, focus, and communicating with others. How many things did you learn from your first job?

I think even if you have a family business, you should work for a corporation or a big company that's not your family business. When you work at an outside company, you get treated like everyone else in the world, and there is favoritism.

"Opportunity is missed by most people because it is dressed in overalls and looks like work." — Thomas Edison

Review check stubs

As the parent, you should sit down with your child and review their check stubs. Take time to explain to them why their paycheck is less than they thought it would be. Doing this can help them bond with you.

Many kids complain that their parents work too much. They don't always understand the difference between household income and household expenses. Conversations like net and gross income can be the beginning of them understanding why you may work so much.

Check stubs have a lot of important details like all the taxes, fees, and other withholdings. Show them how to check for mistakes on their hours or pay rate. Companies make mistakes too, and you don't want your child working for free.

Teach them about 401k monies and explain how saving in investments at a young age can help change the direction of their life. They can open retirement accounts at eighteen years old.

Investing in retirement is a complex subject, but if they know that they need to start as young as possible, that's a good place to start. Let their questions guide the talk from there. Answer what you can, and let the Internet help you with the rest.

"Employees, especially young people, want more than a paycheck." —Marissa Mayer

Explain income taxes

Once you have used their check stub to show them the taxes coming out, you can have another talk about taxes. Explain to them what types of things the government uses the tax money for. You can talk about road replacement and repair, school teachers' salaries, and government officials' salaries.

You can also explain to them about tax season, which is from January 1 to April 17. Talk about the process of filing taxes and what it means to get a refund or owe the IRS. You can even explain to them what the IRS is and what they do.
As a teen worker, they can file their taxes, even if you claim them on your taxes. Sure, the money they get back in refunds won't be a lot, but it's better than nothing.

I would suggest that parents go with their teen to the tax preparers office because there are some questions that if not answered correctly can affect the parents' taxes as well. Make sure the teen goes to the tax office too so that it is a learning moment.

"Everything is complicated if no one explains it to you." — *Fredrik Backman*

Just Start Doing What It Takes

If you learn nothing else from this book, please start teaching your children about money now. I know for some parents this whole topic of money can be taboo. I understand that your parents may not have taught you about money. Neither did mine, but that's okay.

Don't make excuses; start showing them today. It's okay not to know all the answers. The Internet can help you answer questions you don't know the answer to.

Money management is a learned skill. The more you expose your children to different concepts of money, the more they will flourish in this topic. As parents, we don't have to have all the answers, we just need to have the right questions.

Today we have so many ways to find the correct answers to our questions.
You can read blog posts, listen to podcasts, and watch videos. Send me emails at info@mylittlebanker.com for help with your money questions.

"To improve is to change; to be perfect is to change often." —Winston Churchill

Teach Money Daily

Talk to your children about money every day and use real-life opportunities to teach them money concepts.
A few months back my son asked me where I was going, and I replied, "To the bank." He asked me why I was going to the bank and I said, "To pay my rent." Then he asked what rent is.

I explained that where we live is not free and I have to pay rent every month for us to live there. The next month I took my sons with me, and they participated in the whole process. We went to the bank to get a cashier's check. Then we went to the leasing office. I let one son give the office manager the check, and the other got the receipt.

Although only one son was asking me rent questions, it was a great learning experience for both. Now they both understand rent.
Finding ways like this to tie in money lessons makes the process a little easier and not so overwhelming. This way you are giving them bite-size lessons that all add up to something big later.

"True life is lived when tiny changes occur." — *Leo Tolstoy*

Debit vs. Credit

Teach your child that a debit card is not a credit card. You may find it hard to believe, but this is one of my top questions from teens. I must explain the difference between credit and debit cards.

With debit cards, you are paying the money now with cash you have in an account. With credit, it is a promise to pay the borrowed money back with cash you will have in the future.

I guess teens are embarrassed to ask their parents this simple question. Ask your teen some simple money questions and see what they can and can't answer. Their answers will guide you on what to teach them.

"You want 21 percent risk free? Pay off your credit cards." —Andrew Tobias

One Last Thing

Let them ask you questions and answer the ones you can. If you don't know an answer, you can find it together. That experience of you and your child learning together will be etched into their memory.

My father had dyslexia and asked me twenty-three years ago to help him with his written driver's test. I can still remember helping my dad study for his driver's license test and the feeling of pride we both shared when he passed it.

Don't shame your kid and they won't shame you. When doing something new like teaching them about money, make sure not to use mean or hurtful words or wording. Being critical can have a lasting negative effect on a child. They may resent your or money and act out negatively, like getting into heavy debt or overspending as adults.

I want you to know that no matter what your relationship with money is, you can teach your children to have good money skills using the techniques in this book just remember, if you start the conversation about money with them, they will learn from it.

I hope that you have learned a lot and gained some idea on what, when, and how to teach your children about money. I wanted to write this book as a short guide of things any parent can do to start the learning process about money with their child.

This topic of financial literacy is so important today. As parents we want our children to be equipped for whatever they must deal with as adults. Be patient with your learner and have fun.

Play with them and teach them naturally as money subjects come up. Money is not an adult topic—it is a family topic, so start teaching your children NOW.

"Money is only a tool. It will take you wherever you wish, but it will not replace you as the driver." —*Ayn Rand*

Helpful Tools

Join us community to ask your questions and to get support from other parents bit.ly/the25book

Blog Posts:
raeshalsolomon.com/money-blog/

It's Time to Teach Your Daughter to Be Money-Smart
http://sumo.ly/zk8N

The Best Way to Teach Your Kids About Money
http://sumo.ly/HomP

How to Use Video Games to Teach Kids About Money
https://melissablevins.com/video-games-to-teach-kids-about-money/

Talking to Your Kids About an Affordable College
http://bit.ly/2Mr7Hga

How Can I Teach My Kids About Money?
https://womenwhomoney.com/teach-kids-money/

Simple Vocabulary for Children Ages 4 to 14

Teach you child all the words from this list and then add more words as needed.

Asset
Bank Account
Budget
Credit
Credit Score
Debit card
Debt
Deposit
Entrepreneur
Insurance
Investment
Liability
Minimum Wage
Money
Ownership
Paycheck
Price
Saving
Scholarship
Services
Stock
Stock Market
Tax
Withdrawal

MY LITTLE BANKER
Presents:
Money Lessons Made Fun

The My Little Banker series is a collection of books that help parents teach their children about money. Each book has a money lesson told in a way that the listener can understand. Each book has comprehension questions on the back. Email a picture of form to info@mylittlebanker.com

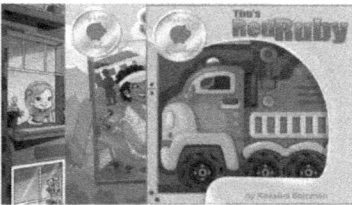

Only $27 for the Set

Gale's Day of Giving
Shop Shop Shop
Tim's Red Rudy

OR

3 books teaching your child about saving, spending and giving

Only $10 for a book

Shop Shop Shop
Or
Tim's Red Rudy
Or
Gale's Day of Giving

1 book teaching your child about responsible spending

First Name: Last Name:

Book Title: Circle One   Payment Method: Credit / Debit Card:

Gale's Day of Giving / Shop Shop Shop / Tim's Red Ruby

Amount Paid: $10 $20 $27   Card Type:

Billing Address:

                                                Card Number:

Zip code: Expire Date: /   /
CVC:

www.mylittlebanker.com

Family Member Name:

For the Week of:

daily Chores

	S	M	T	W	TH	F	S
___	○	○	○	○	○	○	○
___	○	○	○	○	○	○	○
___	○	○	○	○	○	○	○
___	○	○	○	○	○	○	○
___	●	●	●	●	●	●	●

Changing Family Trees Breaking the Generational Money Craze

Visit Mylittlebanker.com/resources for color PDF

Month:

Year:

monthly Budget

Bill / Expense   Amount Due   Amount Paid

Changing Family Trees Breaking the Generational Money Curse

Visit Mylittlebanker.com/resources for color PDF

Name

paper Check

		1547
Pay to the Order of	Date	$
		Dollars
Memo		
123456789 000111000 1547		

		1548
Pay to the Order of	Date	$
		Dollars
Memo		
123456789 000111000 1548		

Changing Family Trees Breaking the Generational Money Curse

Visit Mylittlebanker.com/resources for color PDF

SHARE A PICTURE OF THIS BOOK AND YOUR OPINION OF IT ON INSTAGRAM WITH #MYLITTLEBANKER.

www.ingramcontent.com/pod-product-compliance
Lightning Source LLC
Chambersburg PA
CBHW071012160426
43193CB00012B/2026